Blue Clouds

Blue Clouds

A Collection of

SOUL'S CREATIVE INTELLIGENCE

CAROLYN RIKER

2016

GOLDEN DRAGONFLY PRESS

To Kyle and Genevieve and Copper.
Thank you for your love.

CONTENTS

CHAPTER 1

Nature: Flora, Fauna & Feathers

CHAPTER 2

Soul: Secrets & Sea

CHAPTER 3
Dream within Dreams

CHAPTER 4

Love: Lessons & Latitude

CHAPTER 5

Shadows and Light Are Her Whole

INTRODUCTION

J ust before writing this introduction, I step outside to breathe in a star-filled sky and took a walk with my thoughts. I realized then there probably isn't a proper way to express my deepest gratitude for all of the encouragement I've received to compile this debut book of poetry and prose.

In the last few years, I recognize the immense courage it takes to write a book. I could rewrite, reorder and rearrange this current set of poetry and prose endlessly. And for nearly two years I've tried. Fortunately, my wise friend, mentor and author, David Bedrick, said, "Carolyn, please stop. Let your words go out into the world. This book is done. It's time to start the next one." And with great trust and kind reminders, I did both.

Blue Clouds is an unleashing and synthesis expressing a fertile repertoire of poems and poignant short essays. It is a collection of my soul's deeper creative intelligence. *Blue Clouds* is a unique form of poetic syntax, divided into five pivotal points of inspiration: Nature, Soul, Dreams, Love and Shadows.

Gathered in this selection, I creatively convey an intricate set of emotions and paint images from the last four years of intimate transformation. Every single word sits side-by-side, comforting each other like a dear friend.

I believe in the power of words, the soul of nature, the heart of dreams, and the vibration of music. When immersed together, it teaches the love of real. It is where my voice has a channel; a humanistic activism to express what isn't fully seen, however what I deeply feel.

As poet, June Jordan brilliantly wrote, "Poetry is a political act because it involves telling the truth. In the process of telling the truth about what you feel or what you see, each of us has to get in touch with himself or herself in a really deep, serious way."

Therefore, I hope you'll hold this book closely so we may connect together through the poetic threads of our soul speak.

Much love,

Carolyn

ACKNOWLEDGEMENTS

My list of gratitude is much larger than this space can possibly hold. *Blue Clouds* has a heart inspired by many. Through copious journal entries and endless hours of writing and thousands of pages over the decades, I know writing is my passion and the wild of my sea's voice.

I extend my sincere appreciate to my mentor and dear friend, Catherine (Ghosh) Schweig, founder of *Journey of the Heart: Women's Spiritual Poetry* who breathed encouragement into my hidden poetic wings. On a cold, dark November night, four years ago, I shared a poem, *Message of the Birds*, to her online journal and she graciously accepted it. I hadn't shared a poem with anyone in over two decades. That moment was the continuation of a dream and I haven't stopped sharing since.

Each step of the way, my children, Kyle and Genevieve and our house tiger, Copper have always believed in me. It is their creative spirit, intelligent will, tender love, and of course their wicked sense of humor that keeps me going.

I offer special thanks to my publisher, Alice Maldonado Gallardo, of *Golden Dragonfly Press*, who effortlessly guided me through the publishing process, designing the book cover and patiently answering my questions.

My deep thanks also extends to my friend, Mary Liz Austin and her exquisite photography for the book cover. Her artistry is breathtaking and her humble and generous spirit abounds. I'm beyond grateful.

To my dear close friends, you fill my heart with a deep bow. Each of you have gifted me with insights and loving support. There were some rocky moments and it was *your* words and compassionate listening ear that became my shore.

As Virginia Woolf succinctly penned, "We melt into each other with phrases. We are edged with mist..." Graced with the wisdom of Dr. Maya Angelou, "Nothing can dim the light that shines within you." I believe this is the center of where we begin to see who we truly are.

If you have joined me in anyway on this journey, we are a synergy and an ebb and flow. For that and much more, I am truly thankful.

With deepest respect and love,

Carolyn

Message of the Birds

"....What is here isn't. This is a spiritual quest. It's a matter of seeing between the dot and the blur, the love and the fear. It's a space between a leaf, a flutter and a breeze."

And she knew as soft and real as the moss where she stood, truth and been translated in their song. Life was in motion; awakened and renewed.

CHAPTER I

Nature: Flora, Fauna & Feathers

"Nature is not matter only. She is also spirit."
—Carl Jung

Words and Moments

I have to write when the sun settles into shadows dancing on walls. I write to calm the creases; it distills my heart's song. There's a serendipitous nature of prose when it touches tangential streams.

It is love speaking.

I see words in moments: a nod, a glance and a blink of smile, a tear. We exchange words in the periphery of extraordinary more often than not.

I nestle into and listen between the frost of chartreuse and the sunlight of crisp and the echoes of daydreams. I hold the strings of true and let go of those not willing to.

I weave and dance into the imagination of lithe and free.

Words are there as step stones of unique, priceless and tender.

It is where I find my soul.

Stained Tea Leaves

I'll stitch a poem
with delicate twigs
a nest of budding leaves.

Effortlessly as
crumpled grasses shift
and iris fronds gaze
at sky's deeply felt sea.

The sun softly bequeaths
and rapturous trills reach
the porous eddies of soul
while tree bark
rustles their speak,

Go and rest
let your dreams soak
in amber stained tea leaves
it's our gift
for you to hold.

Hummingbirds

I felt
a thousand hummingbirds
dance
through a rainbow
when sunlight
dusted my lips
and eyelashes.

Bridge of Dawn

It's a prayerful pause
as budding leaves droop,
redbuds weep
a solemn silence accentuates
the steel gray mistiness
at the cusp of nightfall.

Candles lit
one by one
flicker over shadows
seal in the warmth and
bridge the escape of dawn
until a trill
of early birdsong.

Ancient Whale Speak

Usually she had words stacked in steps much like leaves on a tree. She felt settled combing through the archives for just the right scent or flavor of articulation. In those moments she spoke the tongue of ancient whale speak.

However, recent days filled her with a heavy exhaustion. Breathing felt best only sideways under copious pillows and such.

Her skin folded into layers of wispy and her veins were a shade bluer.

She sought shelter in the sound of silence.

Nothingness befriended her between the sleeves of land and sea and there she dreamt of art and books and poems. The shoreline of blankets embraced her weary and hid her soul on the shelves of safe.

Each pause, coaxed her deeper into knowing...

"...if the world has ceased to hear you, say to the silent earth: I flow. To the rushing water: I am."—Rainer Maria Rilke

And there, she felt at home.

Light isn't always buoyant and shadows aren't always despair; yet both, I believe, are limitless in lessons that they share.

Calligraphy of Moon

The finest nib
of quilled pen
engraved
fair fibers
of hallowed sky.

Calligraphy of moon spoke
her voice ubiquitous
as poetry emblazed
on soul's sigh.

Trees Teach Me

"In nature, nothing is perfect and everything is perfect. Trees can be contorted, bent in weird ways, and they're still beautiful."

—Alice Walker

We are similar to trees. Unique and weird and beautiful. Our skin color, like the varied bark of a tree, is a map of contours and shapes. Our arms—the boughs. The leaves—our hair. The roots connect us to a galaxy above and below; we are the heart of veins and interconnected. We can be quiet or outspoken. We can fluctuate like the wind or lay prostrate into the decay of finding our whole. It is in our imperfections, vulnerabilities and expressions of heart —that deeply move us.

My contemplations and questions come from these perennial evergreens: *How can I do better and give more? How can I forgive myself when I fail and learn from my mistakes? How can I see clearly?*

I have to watch and listen and feel. Nature teaches me we are similar to the sea. I am not linear and yet I can get caught in a sticky web of voices and demands and relentless distractions of shallow. This is when I really need to sink below the noise and listen to nature and her trees. It's important to protect myself fiercely with self-nurturing; to trust in the shakedown of confusion because inner truth will rise brighter regardless of any darkness.

Winter is My Companion

Maybe, it's sacred to breathe slower,
walk softer, into the winterish nights
and let it seep into the shortened
days of ancient gray.

Maybe, it's hypnotic to
study the fire's flame
and watch candle lights glow
along an edgeless night's frame.

Maybe, winterberries accent
the fields as crimson reminders
of wild saffron centered violets
as they slumber beneath the bitter chill.

And maybe I have taken
field and form of hibernation
into my cave
a nest of cerulean and opaque hues,
blankets and quilts and softest pillows;
a gathering of tea, the handhold splendor
longing for whispers of fresh snow.

Maybe winter is my companion
and my comfort of much needed silence;
how I embrace her blackest of precious pearls
the graceful midnight's turn of velvet and
down warmth of knowing
rabbits sleep safe and softly below.

Maybe, I am able to burrow next to
my own soul's deepest throes;
my heart aches to replenish and
my mind's prism

is at last able to paint canvas
of infinite sky and speculative wonder.

And maybe, it is sacred to
rest under the artic chill
till springs lightness tugs me forth,
and my aged budding
is once again renewed.

Honey Colored Birds

With great effort,
I pinned
a slice of lemon
to heavy gray skies
and honey colored birds
poured tea
over my storms.

Why Sleep?

It could be a cobalt sky
when sun rises
but for now
ebony ink
spills freely.

Faint starlight dapples
the branches of heavy
while a brilliant moon speaks
thoughts shower shooting stars.

Why sleep
when center is set
to an altered zone
and tidal pools tiptoe
to caves in the deep?

I might just walk
along a beach
and handpick
pink shells
or taste tropical
in the heat
of a coconut cocoon.

I have no worries,
for the moon carries
the sleepless
on her sojourn to full.

I'll tell you a Story

I'll tell you a story, where it's okay that starlight tingles and sea-speak is the golden space between words.

I'll tell you a story where endings are a beginning and the sun can set east because west is too full.

I'll tell you a story where *never* is not forever and silence may hold more wisdom than you can see.

I'll tell you a story where slivers of mental landscape puncture the periphery of deceit and shifts in the wind help to balance the heavy of unsettled.

I'll tell you a story where new only translates what the soul knows of ancient.

I'll tell you a story, far, far from here where blades of grass are fluent in sentient knowledge and trees are a mandala of prayer.

I'll tell this story and maybe, just maybe you'll listen and hear.

Watercolors of Nature

Mist has spun
a sacred signature
inscribed on
soul's bowed branches.

Watercolors arise
from alabaster rime
the fluidity of dreams,
in subtle spaciousness.

While nature composes,
layers of quiet
heart's reflection heals
with compassion.

Feathers of Morning

Winter's circumference translates silence. Ebony brings a blanket of comfort in the stillness of a late rising dawn.

Moon is always there. A half blink of shadow, a crescent of an eyelash, opulent in fullness, spellbound in nothingness, and a friend.

I gather strength in the dormancy of shortened days and deliciously longer nights. I fan inner light with words and music. I listen between an owl's talons and stark sketches of branches against a harsh world. I pour the sands of timelessness across the weeping sea and wipe the estuaries of overflow with eucalyptus leaves.

The waves like the moon whisper, *healing, healing,* into midnight until the first sound of feathers announces a morning song. And I curl around the voices, *be still*; knowing more answers will come.

"*There is something infinitely healing in the repeated refrains of nature—the assurance that dawn comes after night, and spring after the winter.*"

—Rachel Carson

I Became Nature

I became the song of a hollyhock
in the eyes of a reverie
perched on the quiver of vulnerability.

I became a mélange of lilting layers
lightly affixed at the apex of a fluted edge;
my soul covets silence and rest.

I became earth's symphony
drenched in the healing of sacredness
I sensate a hiatus from this arduous odyssey of evolution.

I became a sundial of shadows
liberated by the fragile chrysalis within and
honored the hallowed moonset of tender self-forgiveness.

Rain Soaked Soul

She rested her cheek
against
the cool windowpane
letting the rain
soak through her.

Painted Bluebird

Nature came into her room,
painting a mural
on the wall of shadowy branches.

She become its forest
and effortlessly blended.

She become the music of a
hand painted bluebird
or maybe it was a wren.

Either way,
her song was
and is
hauntingly beautiful.

Unzip the Sky

She snipped clouds
into blankets
to silence the voices
and gathered stardust
to fill her pockets
and anchor her thoughts
as the universe shook;
she unzipped the sky
and rested her head
along the Milky Way.

Bluish Seaweed

I step between the pages of time. It's where my mind curves and my thinking can sift and sort and churn. Layers readjust and revise. Editing along the way to find the key to express the description of time.

I taste the wind. It's the arc above a sunspot and yet the stability of a mountain top. Nature infuses me and brings me words on the wings of birds.

I become the sea and cry rivulets of relief; a dance of nautical bluish seaweed.

I paint the words with expansive strokes instilled on the soul of cell-speak.

For I am finally free to be me.

It is an oasis of beauty to listen to the call of silence; only there in the trees or buds or floral refuge, could she hear the soundwaves of her heart's truth.

Raging Storms

Bring me to the mighty sea
and let my soul
taste the collection of briny tears
of my ancestor's dreams.

Let me grace the waves
of twilight
and greet
her at dawn.

I have storms raging
my veins carry salinity
let the waters soften
my rocky shores
and let not
my words cease.

Flat Stitches on Pale Clouds

Colors
voiced to be seen
in a seamless ashen sky
passionately pursued
flat stitches of pale clouds
her unruly mane,
laughed
while a lemon's twist
slashed between somber
and highlighted
gray's subtle
dazzling brilliance.

Spirits Walk

Lapis lit sky
silhouetted by trees
fingertips of the earth
touch the shrouded haze
I bow in stillness
as spirits walk and
worship with me.

Sometimes, rain weeps the sound of souls.

Scents of Rosemary

How is it,
I hold my breath
forever spellbound
with the setting of the sun?

Scents of woodsy rosemary
chasing dormant lavender
tender new growth extending
for a final sip.

The dimming of daylight
arching to a rest
in a blaze of tangerine.

I close my eyes
and in my veins
I remained tethered
to this dream.

I Must Have Nature

I must
I have to
and I always will
find splendor
in nature
to let my heart
be still.

Trapped Butterfly, Impossible

The snapshots
in my mind
are restless
I need a butterfly net
to capture them
but that
would be like
pinning stars
under a glass case;
it is
impossible.

"There is always music amongst the trees in the garden, but our hearts must be very quiet to hear it."

—Minnie Aumonier

Clematis

I stood next to the window
and leaned against space
time drifting above the trees
cresting with the waves of sunlight.

The salmon pink petals of poppies
were my wings.

A clematis vine tethered me securely
from touching the sun's heat.

Stars flew from the tips of my fingers
and my feet became coiled fronds.

I drank ellipses of energy
from freshly flowing ethereal springs.

And in that fractional space
of orbital bliss,
the velocity of time slowed.

For the edges of awareness
heeded my acute need
for the deepest
healing of
silence.

Rain Between My Fingers

I'll explain
just a little
because otherwise
I'll have to fully open my eyes
and stop the rain soaking
between my fingers
and honestly
I can hardly find ground
for I'm floating with ease
to the tremble of tender leaves
under a soft dance of
nature's wild nectar.

Fluted Notes

In silent blinks
of soft said quiet
I heard
the faintest
fluted notes,
only soul and Moon
could possibly
have heard.

Gifts of Creativity

The winter's nightscape was dabbled with sparks of light. The moon lowered on threads of spun stardust and amplified the cries of the unheard.

I crept closer to hear and held the hand of distress. She was near the creases of eyes and the silence of a whisper and outlined in the corner of yesteryears.

She was the sequel in the gifts of creativity.

I watched as she rocked softly to a hum no one could hear and stroked the funnel of fears. Music played in the layers of her mind and the soul of her planets orchestrated time.

As the edges opened, a depth of a weathered rock appeared and waves of midnight washed gifts on the shore of her heart.

She was transposing life's darkness from threads of stardust into cloaks of empathy and love.

Shadows

I'm softly pressed
into the earth
my shadowy sides
turned inward
soundless
is seeded
in awareness
only then
can I hear
my heart's
worth.

Curve of a Raindrop

Sometimes,
I hear music
in the
curve
of a
raindrop.

Today there's Only Sepia

When I'm aware, the wind will blow and the trees will sing. The branches will sway and the air will tilt slightly into soft. There is no right or wrong. Usually there's hints of gray and splashes of brilliant greens and they add to the depth of complete.

Although today, there's only sepia and I'm alright with that.

I asked what spirits might be listening, *"How often do we hold onto everything? All the time. Forever thinking we have to?"*

And the trees befell with kindly comfort,

"Let go a little and I'll send a message to all the Willows to weep and the Redwoods to carry and the River Birch to soothe. Let all that you hold drip next to the exhausted rose and over the distant snowy peak of a thought on mountain's edge. Breathe for a few within this safe shelter and bow into the soft darkness knowing there's a connection of everything always with you."

Night Prayer

May words be soft
and music quiet.

May kindness wrap
in the corners of unsure
and sip the tea of self-love.

May honey stir
to the rhythm
of a pillow's heartbeat.

And may you fold
into twilight's
mystical night song

Meet Me

Meet me, at quarter past Moon
where time is an always
of cerulean blues.

Let's watch and be
and see afar,
to feel and heal
humanities crater-like scars.

Let's be the hands of shadow-light
and find the edge-speak
of soul to soul.

I'll be there,
wanting,
leaning,
and learning
with a universal flow.

CHAPTER 2

Soul: Secrets & Sea

"I simply believe that some part of the human Self or Soul is not subject to the laws of space and time." —Carl Jung

Hold me Tightly

It happens in the
the tempo of delicate
and bluebells of shadow's sound.

It happens, unwittingly
when I cease
the always of doing.

It happens in the
unusual, a sequel of dappled lace
and shiver of evergreen's pined grace.

It happens in the
curve of speculative time
soaked in honeyed rain.

It is where words hold me tightly
against rib of heartbeat,
a reunion of soft holy
transparent as conversation with
leafed and winged petal.

It is where
we are magnified
in the springs of our gifted splendor
and seen in the heart-soul of a raindrop's eye.

Infinite and Complex

I don't fully understand how some moments can be so exquisite and others with a flip of a feather, the doors and windows of our psyche can feel the minute explosion of everything. It can be a swift descent and a spiral into something surreal; a movie where the reel of film goes 'click-flip, click-flip,' until a new reel is added.

There's a voice, "Mind the gap please." Until life can proceed where a splice of time was lost and where we might even feel deceived. And yet, we hold onto the threads of something we can't fully see.

We follow the stardust of our beginning. We brush off the twigs of criticism, the fear of failure, the angst of anxiety, while holding a fractured lens of perception. We reach for books and music, and the words of kindness or the quiet cave of small.

Eventually our film will smooth out and we stand to find the ground and hold the walls once rebelling. The day returns to light and the night is an envelope with pinpricks in the parchment to behold the stars.

We settle into our breath and wipe our palms free of confusion to feel and listen to our heart. It's there—*The flutter of a gentle thump repeats: I am. We are.*

We are the individual threads of a connected symphony and we each play a different symbolic instrument to enhance a growing, expanding, contracting world goal. One with multifaceted colors and shades and beliefs to feel and hear and see, an infinite equality in you and me.

Ancient Heaviness

I heard the voices sob
through an undercurrent;
a sordid fog clung to my cells
the grip festered an exchange
of an uneasy heaviness.

I scrapped the barnacles
into a blue dish
and lit a candle
to dance with shadows.

I honored
a bottomless grief
and lowered
my sails
to drift
in the voyage of
my soul's sea.

Softest Quiet

Sometimes
the quietest
spaces
hold the
deepest wisdom
softest kindness
I have
ever
known.

Quantum of Sensitivity

Let's soften for just a few and respect and honor the real in me and you. That exquisite tangled space where we aren't strong or wise.

Where we crumble to see the paradox—

Weakness is our strength,
the tar of our fears is the key.
That space where we tremble
and learn from our mistakes.

It is the real, where soul meets soul,
and bridges the tainted we try to hide;
until we see pure is in the shadow
that carries our light.

It is the holy of our holiest.
The quantum of our sensitivity
and the intimate alchemy
of what we truly desire.

Maybe solitude is the soul's tuning fork. It has a similar sound of tiny tender droplets of set dew.

Primitive Spaces

Muddy,
damp
darkened spaces
unfold in layers
along the wind
a soft rocking
to escape
into a primitive space
near leaves of yesterday
under a sky
painted
in flowering shades of gray
no one can hear
the reversed punctuated stillness
of a perpetual
feverish ache.

Peace Was Seeking Her

The heavy fruited dogwood lowered its branches. Silence was laden and the roots of each tree intertwined in prayer. Rain clouds gathered wearing heavy gray layers; while odd gilded orbs spun magically before her.

Peace was seeking her.

Perched high, next to tawny rinsed leaves, she was wrapped in blankets of autumn's distressed petals of late rose.

The birds softly warbled and one by one they nimbly flittered to soothe.

Soundlessly she awoke from an endless dream where she flew across a vast sea from *Somewhere* to back *Here*.

In the palm of each hand she held a feather and knew:

Life is fragile as it is vivacious. What seems clear is and sometimes isn't.

A symbolic door closed behind her and the birds of peace brought her home.

Webbed Shawl

How I adore the scent
of late afternoon sun
and admire
the spider's webbed shawls
how my eyes know
to squint
and rainbow halos
drench it all.

Deep Silence

I took a nap
in clear blue waters
the sand beneath
was creamy white
for miles and miles
clouds swirled endlessly
suspended into a
deep
deep
silence.

Synchronicities

I'll explore the paradox of still
within the buzz of my thoughts
and the gentle cocoon
of sketching an outline of
now versus what will be.

I'll enjoy the synchronicities of words,
or the way shadows tilt
and fully embrace
musical trills
slipping beneath ordinary.

For I'm fully wrapped
in a semicolon;
holding the dot
and resting in the curve
of my ageless river's words.

Waves of a Revolution

Let's celebrate our giftedness. The quiet and shy, the extroverted and introverted and *side-verted*. I am not you and you are not me and that is beautiful.

We are all creative and have a deeper dream. It's our true voice that gets pushed aside. The one that feels criticized.

There's so much competing and demanding our time. The voices are relentless in an inner and outer war. It might even feel like a revolving door.

Let's stop for a few, to feel the cloud-soft, step-stones of our heart's path.

What burns? What pulls? What makes us rejoice and speak out?

Let's become the gaps between the words and hear the shoreline of our soul-centered waves. Let's wrap a kind quilt over our uneven stiches and tattered holes.

For at least a few minutes, let's listen to our inner voice and ask:

"What makes our heart sing?"

I hear the waves of a revolution.

My Chant

The moon
lights a charcoal sky
cradled by branches,
silence listens
prayerful chants are heard.

Silhouetted in her beauty;
her splendor
has a deep
deep
allure.

I taste the mystical enchantment
a tangible universalism;
it mourns,
through my
celestial pores.

Spirit of Weary

In the sharp corners
of my weariness
light seeped in
warming the
spirit and
casting a
gentle
glow.

Shivers of Joy

Peace became the conduit in a fracture of time. It crept in at a not-so-obvious pace; like songbirds chortling and flittering amid the trees.

It was there and she could breathe.

Sunlight purposefully lifted the clouds for a brief encore and the crocuses were dazzled by a warm spotlight—she could feel the glistening shivers of a porous ecstasy of joy.

It Will Be Okay

The sunset of despair fills her and the sunrise of light turns the tides. She follows and crawls through dark and confused. It is haunting voices and fear of an endless tunnel. She finds a cave with blind fish to swim by her side. She leans into hollow looking for solid. This is where she is on the sunniest of days. Wave upon wave she awaits for the turn of tides.

Because something deep inside knows, it will be okay.

Gentle Escape

I forgot to listen
to the sound of silence
at the first light of dawn
and yet the ocean came to me
in my mug, a gentle roar of waves
tiny elliptical escapes of bubbles tapping,
dancing beneath shades of blue sketching anew,
I held the goblet and stared beyond the frosty leaves
the buds of gentle, were not lost but found within my reach.

When Night Touches Grass

I'm not sure why...
but when the night
touches the grass,
the swallows sleep
and rain
is a chant of
quiet breath
there's a release and
shouldered cries
can be heard.

Your Soul Needs Silence

The sun called her out to play and the petals of faded yesterday swayed. The music of song birds teased the shadows and parted the light. The scent of emerald and warmth of spun-brown nature, filled her; she walked between harsh and discovered the veins of said sorrow. She bowed to her ancestors and they graced her with the gifts of tender and quiet.

She listened to the feathers of thought, *"Your soul needs silence."*

Frost Gilded Rose

Solitude and I walked
between chestnut paths
and cobalt sea skies;
a reverie of shelter,
needed
breath and silence
sun and solace
today, a gifted
frost gilded rose.

Wings Unfurled

Fate would have it, while sifting through soap and suds of ordinary, I became the inky sky. I squeezed the rain and stars fell exactly where my tea steeped.

The sticky-sweet of honey coated the floor and my mind.

I breathed and leaned into a full stretch. My wings unfurled and I soared the sea blue of green and majestic mountains unseen.

I felt a lick of faintest whisper and saw the words on fingertip, *"Follow, follow, follow your soul. She sees your heart sing."*

"Sometimes she did not know what she feared, what she desired: whether she feared or desired what had been or what would be, and precisely what she desired, she did not know."

—Leo Tolstoy, *Anna Karenina*

A Safe Freefall into Comfort Foods

We might need a break every now and then from the assault of living.

We hold space for each other for a variety of reasons. We feel the joy of celebrations and the mixed batch of criticisms and miscommunications. We see and hear and feel and touch into a depth of exquisite pleasures and caustic hurts. We are pulled in a multitude of directions each crying for our attention.

That is when I notice how my mind and heart can no longer hold the fullness of it all. Something in me and around me quivers and I physically begin to ache; my emotions ripple into a dizzy fractal geometric state.

And as I listen to my needs, I'm learning: it's okay to step away from this surface tension. Sometimes we need to curl into dormancy and let the scaffolding around our heart release into the soft sound of pillows.

It's a safe freefall of letting go.

Candles lit and comfort foods are found. I let my mind puddle and hold the blues and the setting sun against my chest and weave prayers in the simplicity of rest.

Befriend the Sea

I'm below sea level,
silt and sand
muted
benevolence
I'll sift
in the sway
as nary
sea form
befriends
me.

Kaleidoscope Jar

I'm on edges of unsettled,
holding butterflies of mysterious,
wrapped in a kaleidoscope jar
of midnight and stars.

Something is amiss
and I wish I could say,
it is this or that
but I'm perplexed
at the intensity
of the undefinable.

It's neither here or there;
sort of a paradox
and a parallel split in time's
spacious and watchful eye.

So I lean into quiet
as much as I can
and listen to the song of silence.

Maybe there,
stardust will sleep
into spaces
and comfort my inner shift;
inside the prisms of my mind.

Barely Surviving

I'm not
of this
world
it pains me
deeply
so each night,
just to survive,
I snip a piece of
mountain,
sea or sky
and fly.

Variations of Shadows

It might lift
the heaviness
the breath of cement
shadows disintegrate
into eerie and endless.

It will ease
where creases only deepen
rest discovered in tiny branches
on mossy bough to avoid
voices of interrogation.

It's truly fickle,
these variations of shadow
crossing bridges of empty
an unknown destination
of trusting a hellish voyage.

Betrayal still lashes a fierce wound
where grieving archives of burnt pages
and memories are awakened;
it's tragic rewriting a worn pattern
and terrifying to see expansion of anew.

And still, the fickle unease will settle
into a looking glass outward because
inward and surreal will taste real;
healing will be subtle or jolting or not
as the walk with soul's water
continues to seek and renew.

Dew of Compassion

Rest deeply, tenderness of heart
beneath the stardust of hope,
the dew of compassion,
the rekindling of trust
and the blessings
of ancient
souls.

I Breathe a Little Easier

I breathe a little easier when I see how sun and shadow wrap a tree. I walk with the trunks and branches. We become one. Sky meets earth and mountains tremble.

Maybe just maybe trying to figure it-all-out, is a way to hold on. Or maybe the rise and fall of panic is a way to release. Maybe, dormant seeds of sealed secrets will transform. Maybe those short sweet sunspot sleeps, are infused with self-love.

I breathe a little easier when I turn the outer dial way down and let abnormal be my normal. I see crimson, pomegranate and a lemony zest of succulent creativeness; it's my well of madness.

Maybe, for now I'll sail away into quietness, knowing my words are tired and thoughts are heavy but I can still hear the foghorn and know there's a-light-in-the-house.

My anchors are the four corners of Vayu and sound.

I breathe a little easier when I meditate knowing darkness and light are the shadows of a tree always, always with me.

To Find Our Holy

It comforts the way the sun always sets or how rain showers the soul an octave or two below middle C.

It is predictable how the room shifts and the shadows remain.

We need to rest when aches can't breathe and tears get snagged on sleeve.

We linger lower and stretch deeper just knowing to follow the rhythm and find our holy.

It's the decibels in the encore of rain and glass and sea.

It's the emerald taste of an evergreen.

It's the soothing brown of naked earth.

I believe and hope we all discover the anchors of nothingness and find love in the chaos where sand and wind sift away the voices to find our intimate holy...

Just before we drift off and sleep.

CHAPTER 3

Dream within Dreams

"Hold fast to dreams
For if dreams die
Life is a broken-winged bird
That cannot fly.
Hold fast to dreams
For when dreams go
Life is a barren field
Frozen with snow."
—Langston Hughes

Where Democracy Rises

It starts with a sensation,
usually beneath the breastplate
that space unseen but felt
the tear spot of infinity
the raw and real of humanity
where noise is quiet
and solitude echoes a voice;
trees always hear
and the sea breathes through
the stretches and curves
of intuitiveness
until
vocal chords
contract and breach
the consciousness
simultaneously tears tremble with sea
this
to me
is where democracy rises
soul to soul
and we see.

Sleep

My eyes,
oh so heavy,
softly fade
respite of slumber awaits
my mind
delights to unfold
into a collective stream
of unforeseen glyphs
to unravel the secrets
of my soul.

Stars of Pleiades

Once upon a time, there was woman who had a dream and in that dream she was given a message: *"You are not from here. You come from the Stars of Pleiades, the Seven Sisters. Your lesson is to learn and teach and share."*

Within her dream, she glided through passageways of vintage glass carrying a most unusual umbrella. The mist skipped beats and with every splash there was a cymbal of sentient solitude. She was hypnotized as memories dripped off into a slight wind.

Captivated by the soft tempo of rain, she watched as it shimmered between clouded chords. An evolution unfolded so rapidly it was intimidating and unnerving. Everything was a part of a fibrous network similar to the roots and branches of trees. All of us, engaged in a fine synaptic connection of intelligent vibrations living in a harsh world rupturing from negativities.

However, powerful forces were creating an uprising; *a conduit of awareness, activism, truth, love and kindness—an outspoken resolve to end the darkness of injustices.*

She awoke with such a sense of longing and blinked through tears of a deeper understanding. She steadied herself against an invisible force and bowed to the quest of her dreaming-heart-voice. Knowing change isn't easy. Our journey and dreams are perplexing and revealing and one that will thankfully persist for a lifetime.

Dreams within a Dream

Today has drifted from darkness
to shadows of variegated slate
an ancient dense hazy space
trees punctuate the edges
mountains are ghosts
above and below
are clouds
I'm heavily tilted
to the right and
to my left
I belong not here or there
It's a dream within a dream
awareness becomes the edge
and words are written on my soul.

A Saturated Curl of Moon

I tried to capture the moon on film and heard, *"Please don't. Instead, dream about me in words."*

I smiled into the crisp of the setting dew and the scent of air filled my eyes anew.

I listened to the branches speak and her light afar became a saturated curve of a curl, lifting me just above a swirl and resting on a star.

Her stature was noble and quiet and strong. I listened between the shiver and time wasn't lost but stillness became a sea of security. The background noise faded and the lights of artificial dinned.

Cold became warm. Nothingness became real.

The trees framed her poetic glow—what my camera-eye had failed to see.

And as I walked away, still gazing at her serenity, she blinked with waves upon waves...

Tears of moon dust graced me.

Rise

Mist, gracefully shrouds
the morning sun
fragments of dreams
a cadence of light rain
the footsteps of faeries
mystically stills my heart;
enchanting prayers
offered in this sacred space
I peacefully breathe
the cool damp air
as it teases and
dances through the trees
a playful exchange
of wind
sunlight sees the shadows
memories cleansed
by the morning dew
a hazy world
of seeing the past
stepping into new
grateful
as I watch
my heart
rise with the sun.

Deep Intimacy of Stillness

Short of normal. She defined that loosely because it depended on the way the sun was setting or how the trees bowed poignantly. And yet, when at all possible, she became one with the sanctuary of tender and nature.

To the west were songbirds and to the east was the sound of light through filtered trees.

Wind became the waves in solidarity's sea and ancestors were the voices of sprightly springs.

The stillness brought her deep intimacy.

She slipped past sharp and harsh and settled humbly in the greens of budding flora.

In this cyclical daydream, it helped to navigate typical normalcy; for just a few, pressure was lifted, and her wings took flight and she flew.

It's Always a Dream

A dry drink of silence
sequestered in light's breeze.

I putter and unfold and reach
into a sentient daydream.

And tasted syllables of
dawn and feathers of still.

While parting sage pages
to release my ink's spill.

The Girl in a Yellow Dress

I saw her today. We sat in a distant memory. Quietly I watched her contemplate the universe; she held it in her eyes.

The cotton dress appeared sunny and her hair firmly tied until she could set it free. She might have been about three. The apple of youth had fallen too soon from her favorite tree.

She sat closely with the stars and felt the earth move through her feet. Nothing could take her from her daydreams.

Each blink was in rhythm; I felt her breath remove a pane of glass from my heart.

And in the softest voice I could find in my mind I told her how much I loved her. She whispered back with eyelashes laced in morning dew, *"I love you too. I'm glad we made it this far."*

The difficult thing about sleep
is even in my dreams I write.

Shelter the Shadows

I'll paint the sky
with symbols
and let the sea
mitigate the memories.

I'll let the sun
shelter the shadows
of dark blue.

I'll sprint with
the trees
and find silence
in the landscape
of forbidden.

Each wing
turns a wrinkled page
of fibers frayed
it expands and contracts
an invisible filament of force.

It's uneasy to cross
a ghost-like bridge
when real and illusion
are unsure.

Therefore, I'll hold
the strength of knowing
and ease back
to a patch of
just here
in this moment.

Autumn and Letting Go

Morning and night the unfolding of autumn wraps a nudge,
taps my shoulder, and whispers through the bed linens.

I pull warmth closer. I sense the scent of change.

The austere eclipse of summer passing.
The pages I thought I'd write.
The lists I willed to accomplish.
I didn't.

And in the stillness
I walk with shadows and plant seeds.
I water my soul with the clouds.
I taste a mountain and let my soul rinse through a prism.

I have grown.
My lists have too; they always will.
My fingers play on the keys of a pulse and a rhythm of
eccentricity.

I have lost and gained and cherished
the simplicity of seeing the nesting of nature.
I mined for golden orbs and dug deeper into fresh springs of
solitude.

I nurtured more readily the art of, NO to the request of more to do.
I listened when my spirit dissolved into particles
and walked along sentient riverbeds.
I found sand and seaweed dusting my eyelashes,
for my dreams exposed a world.
Maybe, just maybe...
I accomplished more
by letting go.

Under the Sycamore Tree

Join me under the sycamore tree and by the river of life.

Let's walk along the winding path and see the reflection of silent moon. Join me in earth's song where the splendor of trees sing and the dim of light is still bright. Come with me to the center of nothing and skirt the dawn of day. Let's celebrate the flickers of needed dormancy with the heated flames of alchemy. Let's support the sheaths unfolding and not abandon the darkness of souls under siege.

We'll walk together and it'll be okay.

I'll meet you under the sycamore tree of my dreams.

Pointillism of Silence

Night came
with such simple serenity,
I surrendered into breath
of pointillism;
where silence is liquid
and thoughts continue
as dreams.

Silent Affection

I carry words
at the bridge of heart
crossing through a soft sonata.

A wave of wind,
crescendos
trees play the harp
of sea.

I hold the breath of soul
spent in silent sorrow
lifting on the cusp of seeing.

Intimate colors
swarm through the heavens
golden, tart amber
soak the reflections
in the ripple of a dispersed memory.

The translation is wordless;
felt at the breastbone
of torn youth.

It is a dream within a dream
crossing from always
releasing
into night's vessel
of affection.

Lucid Dreams

She drifts to the nearest soft spot
blanket wrapped tightly
pillows hush sounds
recumbent
in a semi-silent-solace
she's shutting down
recalibrating
breathing through a tunnel
time is suspended
letting her
stop
walls turn glass and
extend into nature
sky meets sea
inoculated
from a stream of noise,
she slips off into
a lucid dream
where peace breathes.

Moon Nectar

The moon
in her half fullness
resting on nothingness
the seen and the silence of quivering darkness;
she speaks to me.

She teases the tendrils of thoughts spilling
and words tangled in the depth of distant starlight;
the intensity of energy quickens by day and night
I feel her graceful beams
reach clarity of insight.

The flipside of the moon
the half hidden shadows
lit by dreams we remember
and memories we can't forget;
she captivates an inner glow
and awakens our candidness.

I am the moon and she is me
we dance a rhythmic melody of ebb and flow;
our mysterious femininity unfolds
and age becomes our gifts
as lush as a ripened mango.

The moon
in half her fullness
echoes the waves of the sea
the song of storm and tranquility;
tonight, I will tip a moon slice into my cup
and let her nectar trickle over me.

"I'm in the mood to dissolve in the sky."

—Virginia Woolf

Her Soul as a Dreamer

Sunny rays of amber and gold
sifted through her lashes.

She believed in love
held onto the wisps
and felt the stir of moonlight shifts.

As the years prevailed
tattered, twisted and trivialized
perceptions altered.

Her free-spirit, turned to ebony
weather-worn, chastised and achy.

The illusion of love was deeply torn
the silver lining
was tarnished and forlorn.

And into the safety of her shadows
she dipped deeper,
until a passion to live released her.

She would no longer conform
or bend to the point of breaking
she set her creative intuition free.

She accepted her soul as a dreamer
one foot in this world
and another in a rapturous sea.

Unraveled

Foggy mornings
are a bridge
when sleep
is no longer rest
but thoughts
need a safe
place to
unravel.

We are Worthy

"I tore myself away from the safe comfort of certainties through my love for truth—and truth rewarded me."—Simone de Beauvoir.

I settled lightly on the edge of a dream and began to soar. Between closed eyes the terrain became waves upon a golden shore. Mammoth ethereal wings brushed my skin and I was lifted high above to see a timeline sketched in the sand dunes of my mind.

The past was a devastating richness of mishaps, heart-crushing lessons, experiences and the vitality of surviving. It's all laced with opportunities to transform the mundane and exceptional and tragic into the purpose of gifts to be shared.

The alchemy has been happening all along. Our metamorphosis takes on different shapes.

It is as necessary to lay with heavy wet mulch as it is to rise and risk and expand and fly. Change is always happening even when we are stuck and where edges are conflicted and nothing seemingly makes sense. Somehow though, people believe in us and we begin to recognize own unique empowerment; it embraces the purpose of heart.

We step into the now and not the never. We uphold an inner trilogy of:

We are worthy. We are loved. We are powerful.

And this is the part that really grabs a few dozen tissues from an endless zenith of heart:

We are capable to do anything.

We will shake the stratosphere of constraints; especially to those who say, "No, we can't!"

We will no longer be at the end of a leather lashing of lies. We will no longer be restrained in a suffocating head grip of silence. We will challenge with a warrior stance of integrity and strength.

Our stress fractures begin to heal each time we believe in our self.

We are unfolding a process; it is found in the gifts of our own personal magic.

Things I believe...

It takes time to trust. Not everyone is trustworthy. I wish I didn't care so much, but I do. My sensitivity needs extra quiet space. Pain is real. Cinnamon ice-cream comforts. I cry quietly. Hands can be gentle or not. Intelligence means little, without kindness. I cherish connections and avoid superficiality. Eyes speak. Violence permeates. Hate is real. Wisdom can be found in a rock, the sea or a tree; it is limitless. Respect is necessary. Animals always know. I love to listen and absorb tiny details. To be heard is priceless. I often daydream. Nature soothes. Reading is essential. Healing is perpetual; it is an alchemy of finding our soulfulness. To be loved, feel loved and accepted is one of the most beautiful experiences. And when I doubt or find it hard to breathe, I seek the stars and the sky's eyes remind me: love is infinite.

Softest Shades of Spice

I walked through nutmeg, cinnamon and cloves. These are the earthy tones and flavors of subtle spirits. I held them gently as the feathered flight of a bird. I was carried to a land of diminutive and still. Vertical and horizontal didn't exist. My pores became air and shadows and light didn't fight. It wasn't peace or hope or silence. It was nothingness. I welcomed it with the deepest of gratitude. I closed my eyes knowing, the softest of voices cherish being heard.

Ode to Georgia O'Keeffe

At the dusk of day,
Georgia O'Keeffe
beckoned me.

My heart quickened
to behold the allure,
and witness petals
of a poppy.

She spoke confidently,

"Look closely at the ebony-blue core,
such complicated beauties,
embedded layers
a folded cosmic expansion,
emulating the sky of night
seas deep and earth raised forth....
remember,
it's all within you."

*Night is the mirror of sound; it
pours over the bedding of dreams.*

Colors Seen

When trees call, I listen. It's been that sort of night-morning. First the stars and now charcoal trees stand quietly; almost as if I'm moving through a black and white image.

The sun has yet to rise but the sky is a gorgeous layer of milk and flannel gray. There's a hint of movement and muted colors and crunch of things unseen.

This space is a continuation of my night dreams; a delineated timeline of birth, marked on a long scroll. I hold the thoughts of night and let the dreams unfold into the branches of this changing snapshot of colors seen.

Moss Lined Jewels

In the tangible distance, a spiraling sphere appeared between the edges of raised sunlight and before the shift of silence. It was mystifying and a little unreal.

Voices filled crevices and a blush of nature became a doorway of whispers. Without much thought I stepped in to listen. It was another world's intuition; a sequence of moss-lined jewels written by ink of lavender stems and petals of rose.

There, next to still leaves, flowed rivers and spirits arose. The light of sweet dark and the frail speed of sound froze. The absurdity of it all was indelibly beautiful.

Something though, maybe it was a crow or the way hummer's speak or the way the wind blew but I knew, I had to walk through moss-lined jewels of dappled dew. However, I left a twig of gold to visit again soon.

Ginger Stained Sky

The enveloped edges
of a ginger stained sky
sealed the corners
of nightfall
it pulled me
to places
far
far
from here
and so,
I had to go.

Our Inner Wiser Voice

A wiser self, resides in each of us. Waiting for us to listen.

Last night I heard her whisper in the dark sharp shades of breast and bone.

"Your heart aches of fears and worries from tender to fierce. There's a roar and a compelling compassionate river. I hear you in the dead of soul searching and the quiet of longing. I feel you in the space between songbirds. It hauntingly pierces the incessant unknowns.

Keep stepping forward. Challenge the norms. Let the overwhelm rise and fuel the passion for a deeper societal change. Let each voice join in the variegated beauty of uniqueness. Scrape the cartilage of pressure and seek hollowed wings and soar.

It's painful to be weighted by ordinary and unable to explain the capacity and layers above and beyond. It is challenging to continue into the unknown without someone to rest upon.

However, you must keep moving forward. This life isn't a mistake. It is equally as necessary as those before and yet to come."

CHAPTER 4

Love: Lessons & Latitude

"...Silently the birds
Fly through us.
Oh, I, who long to grow,
I look outside myself,
and the tree inside me grows."
—Rainer Marie Rilke

Blue Bleeds Softly

I no longer have
to explain why today
is so tender or
how vulnerability is tied
to stinging nettles
or how too much is
over my cusp
and even the weight
of blue bleeds soft
I no longer have to
give to extol your gain
for I am complete
with the breath
of feeling on the
wings of forever
and the flowers
will forget-me-not.

This is Love

To feel loved, to be loved and to give love, is a transparent offering.

To be seen and heard, is without a doubt, remarkable.

To listen and hear, priceless.

When we love, we show it. We find words and ways. We set aside time. It's not a chore. We don't try to destroy or change the person into someone else. We let them be an individual. We don't stop their growth; instead we rejoice in their being.

To be loved, we are accepted for who we are. Vulnerability is poignant. Raw is real.

To be loved and to love, takes courage. To be fully seen is incredibly rare and breathtaking. We lower our masks and see a celestial inner being. It is our full self—the supernova as well as the black holes. Our fears and doubts. Our anger and joy.

We witness the expansion and the unknowing parts of our self in safety. This is love.

Naked Thoughts

I asked you,
the other day
what it meant to be
intimately a *we*?

You didn't stop or look
but I saw a brown iris roll
and a page turned mind
shake, a loud *no*
while you aired, a stale joke.

Naked in my thoughts
I still laughed and
asked again
this time you
pushed back
a stack of heavy
hitting my inner floors.

Memories,
coincidently collided
I contemplated
for a decade
the *you* in the *we*
wasn't capable to confide.

I and you were
souls separated
long before
the ink was signed
a turnkey
of beginning and end.

We entails
companionship,
coupled with compassionate
consideration of what
I and *you*,
want and need
the *you*,
could simply not afford.

Inner Voice

I let you into my heart;
a secret sacred space.

My trust in you was assuredly there.
I prayed, it wouldn't be misused.

I gave pearls of veracity;
melodiously wrapped
within my quiet self.

We were parallel lines drifting;
no longer converging but repelling
my synergy fully depleted.
I could give no more, knowing
superficial corrodes my intuitive helm.

My soul lamented,
until I finally understood
I must navigate the depths
of the stars, land and sea.
My time had come
to return to my dreams
and be me.

"Love takes off masks that we fear we cannot live without and know we cannot live within."

—James Arthur Baldwin

We Are Love

All that is love is not always spoken,
It is felt by the trees, sea, wind and earth.

Love is a tempest and when broken,
the shattered discourse will quiver a rebirth.

Heartache will ignite a mystical mend,
from the darkest scripts, folded, shattered and torn.

We grasp at the depths of our spirit and bend,
rising stronger and clearer, no longer forlorn.

Letting go of the illusions, we embrace a galaxy,
a nebulous of intense creative love.

Seeing our existence as stardust, isn't a fallacy,
to be loved, to feel love is infinite as a rising dove.

"I hold this to be the highest task for a bond between two people: that each protects the solitude of the other."

—Rainer Maria Rilke

Peeled Apple of Moon

I peeled an apple
from the core of the moon
and licked the juice of its honey dew.
While ferns feathered a canopy,
I chased the sun
in liquid form
and ribbons of lava were born.

Oh morning moon
where timeless is ordinary
and thoughts are clipped to line
for wind to dry.

I could no long tell
if clouds were waves
or sky was sea;
moon's dawning light
had rushed
to my infinity.

So I spoke to you
and said soft things
like how a whisper
becomes a faded memory;
and you answered
and held this space parallel
to the flicker of morning's grace.

Spirits in Tears

Yesterday,
I wrote of wings and flight
I fancied a journey along wind currents
today,
I am opalescent
stirring wind chimes
with my toes in the sky
I seek harmonies
as leafy winds blow
my brand isn't easily gathered by ordinary
for unimaginable wild tugs at me
my throat voice spills at ruptured justice
and my searing heart
it is not folly nor foolish
I feel spirits in tears
love in soul's sea
evermore in trees
and mountain of stature
voices weep to be heard
I will not be branded to write
just of contentment
for I am a wild seed
with infinite choices.

Ecstasy

A cool spring breeze
tends to unravel me
in the morning light
amid stillness of
budding flora
and spreading leaves;
an uninhibited
ecstasy of soul
in rhythm with
sodden soft steps
as I drift deeper
into nature's folds.

Patch of Peace

It takes one more breath
to find the light between the trees
and the halo of sunset.

It takes one more walk
through longish grass
and mossy strands
to find a patch of peace.

It takes another breath
to soak up the moon's light
and sit with the still of her glow.

It takes a slight breeze to translate
a canopy of trees into an echo
and know,
it's safe.

It takes time to believe
there's more in the shedding
and seeing the gifts we bestow.

Shadowy Bluffs

The braided twist of her hair was more likely a twist seeking love and compassion. The quest flowed from her heart center. The scars that brought her this far were a deep chasm of penetrating shame. She no longer tried to push it aside. Her feelings relinquished on the rocky beaches and unfolded continuously; it astonished her as she walked along the quiet deserted coast. She rode the waves of an immense sea and for ages was struck on a battered barrier reef.

Her stories were rarely spoken but lived in secret cells of memories unknowingly waiting to be released; a safe net of liberation is hard to discern when lies, like broken shells, are perpetuated. She discovered tiny coves of respite to heal and transform the shadowy bluffs delineating the coastal past into fortitude and veracity. Time had lapsed as her feelings shimmered on the current calm of the sea's setting sunlight and the feel of the rise of the moon.

Each painful undertaking to untwist the twisted messages astonished and gratefully assisted in her journey. She embraced her realness; no longer shunning her feelings and began to believe her stories voice. The former chapters eroded the tarnished misgivings into abundant and insightful gifts.

Celtic Songs and Dragonflies

I had to take my words for a stroll today. Out of my mouth and along a river's edge. We gathered under the tallest of trees. Robins and meadowlarks sang Celtic songs and dragonflies danced along. We walked away from the normal and bridged a crescendo of lyrical and lush. Sunlight captured the time between the spaces of unseen. I peeled a few dormant vowel sounds and held the ripe of today in my hand. And wrapped myself around the cherry blossom of antiquity. My writer's thoughts were lifted tenderly above the horizon and I started to see. I felt them in my eyes behind my dreams. It is a place wary of speech and yet keenly felt at the depth of sea and sky and eventually rinses in the sound of virtual ink.

Our World is Ruptured

I retreated to my tiny garden yesterday to listen to the earth and to her unfurling. I raked and trimmed. I felt my mind go quiet behind the daffodils. Earth's musty smell of brown and gray and green commingled freely. Branches accented with new growth and mossy-grass combed over from relentless rain. Taupe stems of hollyhock bowed above spent lavender wands.

All appeared in the deepest of prayer. I walked softly between this sacred grave between dead and new until it began to translate.

"Our world is ruptured. There's more than an undercurrent of angst. Many of us feel and hear it daily. Our world is in profound pain. Even in silence there's a pulse of anguish. Water has turned poisonous through the pipes of injustice. People are being fed lies. Leaders are fighting each other. Racism's spirit remains deafeningly alive. However, more are being awakened and solidarity is being renewed. Trust, is the seed planted to propagate into new."

I stood in my tiny plot—a speck on this planet. All I could think of is the enormous responsibility to continue to connect and write and speak. My heart hurts and more tears come in my night and daydreams. And I know, as seasons change, all of this is a continuous rebirth of my soul's deepest calling.

Transparent hummingbirds flew from her heart and mouth; each bestowed tiny seashells laid lovingly abreast where her soul's shy nakedness grew.

Rosehips of Beauty

I listen to the roses in my garden. Some carry rosehips of beauty. Others are upright and sharp. Some are heirloom and others, carefree. Poignant spots of colorful celebration scattered between the lavender, phlox and whatnot.

Today I'm a rose in a prespring interlude. There's tenderly emerging leaves of growth. My soul's cane is etched in mahogany and my shadowy branches tap the windows of my mind. The moon highlights and the sun warms. The trellis of quiet is an essential anchor as a rose is timeless.

It's the Simple Things

I embrace more and more
to find my center
how the sun touches lavender blues
a gentle breeze tips the silver of green leaves
the sudden kindness of a stranger
how when everything feels tilted,
until I stop
waiting for me to see
the fluctuating dips
are just as symbolic
as the days
I eat clouds with my toes
or sip sunshine from a gossamer straw
it is all very real
as the plunge into icy
is as shocking
as running through fiery hell
I'm so grateful when words can find me
and anchor my pores with
handfuls of warm sand
while the waves
slowly kiss
my crumpled pages
and I can breathe once more.

Mug of Love

Morning came
with silent stain of sun
I heard,
before it spoke
in the stir
of rumpled sheets.

My eyes
hesitant to see
longing to savor the narrow space
where obscure and weightless roam
while softly pulsating to my awake.

I worshiped the scent of coffee beans,
the grind and swirl
a warmth of mahogany
wrapped as daylight gave its birth.

I drank not only a mug of love
but of sounds and feelings and
nature held within.

With pause of breath,
I released silent prayers
and let the rapture of morning,
further seep in.

Meadows and Holy Places

She visited holy places
meadows
open and free
spiraled staircases
by the sea
leading to
vaulted endlessness
glass windows
grew wild and free
she pressed them open
and soared through the clouds
sentient and steadily
she touched the tips
of tender stars
to be gently received
by a divine oasis
of meadow and
holy places of the sea.

Crumpled Wings

It seemed years
she walked alone
weaving a web
around her soul.

Her shoulders taut
as she carried
crumpled wings
and countless souls
until she
let them
go.

Thorns Altered

She became the soil
and earth befriended
dormant lavender
brushed her pulse
cells awakened
nudging her soul
less despised,
unfurled from little repose
honey of nectar,
filled her veins
razor-edged thorns altered
anguished tendrils
into a resounding voice
of verdant leaves
lifted into prayer
tears descended
to her roots
a soothing
witness of
love.

Dissolved

Words,
barbed wired
and rusty spears;
it's harsh to touch
the embers of fiery fear.

Linear dissolves
when wind
kicks raged flames
and tears douse the shame.

We die each time
a branding iron
penetrates our soul.

We regenerate
each time
a tender
herbal balm
rests
on the holy of
jagged edges.

Rewriting,
re-scripting
ligament's memories
and heredity's cells of survival.

We live with our demons
until we befriend them
or die fighting alone.

A Love Story in 108 Words

I didn't ask
to fall in love
but I did
I wasn't looking
and there
you were.

We laughed with ease
I listened,
engaged,
entranced
I held your words
in my cells
my heart breathed.

Time passed
control is stealthy
tumultuous demands
shadowy storms revealed
the pictures hung
tilted
spilling
pain
we changed.

We gave
but rarely enough
to satiate an emptiness
silent, manipulating and cold.

I snipped the chords,
stale air escaped

and strings floated
tinted colors returned
solitude sips tranquility

I didn't expect
to find love, again
but there it was
in my reflection
breathing self-love.

The Sky was painted in Layers of Love

A sliver of blue
slate and white
I felt the setting of the sun;
underneath a veil of clouds
the air,
electrifying
a silent Om touched my skin
eyes sealed,
a rapture of love
descended and held me.

I folded into the galaxies,
the stars
tangled my hair
the four winds
tethered to my limbs
delicate fibers stitched a lattice
of symmetry.

Weaving, assimilating
and assuring me
to the very center
of my heart
this pilgrimage
expands into
the layers of
stardust
and love.

I'm Sorry

I'm sorry,
would have helped
but it was given
with hollow
and I felt the empty
and saw what
love isn't
and how much
we weren't.

And now,
although free
sometimes this hurt
comes in and swallows
the hard cry
still inside of me.

Glass Shards

I watched forever
and hoped you'd see me.

I spoke
you didn't hear.

I leaned in
held the thoughts
streaming.

But each step closer
became punctuated
glass shards against heart.

I needed to protect
from bleeding
my unseen being.

And only then
did my
heartbeat
restart.

I Hold a Sea

I can only pour
one cup
of me
into your arms
because
I hold a sea
and I don't want
the waves
to drown
either you
or me.

Tears

My tears
don't have to
make sense
sometimes
I just
become
the sea.

Pieces of Heart

With each word,
I share
there's a little
part of me;
it's not
just words,
it's my heart.

Finally I Grieve

I was okay
until
I heard
your voice;
my heart
shattered,
not because
I missed you
instead,
I could finally
grieve what
we never
had.

Beds

She left
the beds
unruly
because each
still had
a signature
of human warmth;
that she couldn't bear
to disturb.

97 Colors of Me

He expressed
his love
to her
only when she was
happy
witty or joyful
in her silence
she thought,
"But what about
the other
97 colors
of me?"

Piano

One light lit
she touched each
highly sensitive note
held by ebony and ivory
a dualistic and melodic sonnet
ascended from an infinite cavern
to cease a steady edgy murmuring
of a weighty dissonant storm
she struggled to blend
into accordance of
each rise and fall
the keys spoke
and the music
was able to
reach her.

Why?

Sometimes,
there are
no words for a
visceral feeling;
it simply soaks in
like a cold beating rain and
leaves the questions
dangling into an endless
why?

Quiver of Aliveness

I folded into the crest of dawn
the scent of day called my name
before my shelter had yet to stir.

Still drowsy,
from meadow of fragrant lavender
light bending into waves of rosemary
my skin somehow draped
with a hint of sage and verbena.

White sheets creased into each breath,
dissolving into softness,
leaving footprints of memories
in the shadows of echoes and dew.

I felt the quiver of aliveness
pause at my breastbone
as I shared in the union of solitude.

Read Me like Braille

I want the touch
of gentleness
serene but justly held
of hands, vibrant
reading me like braille
each curvature
and silhouette
a muse of enlightenedness
not afraid of my darkness
or light of slight smile
hidden in crinkles
of lavender's promising hue.

We'd rest, side-by-side
beneath the stars
or near a river's bend
at the peak of a mountain
or nary sea's within
with loving eyes to look upon
my tousled eclectic ways.

I want to feel the breath of
morning mists
or saline visions,
to speak of memories,
mixed with dreams
and craft sandy dunes anew.

I want love
to whisper softly
and fill crescendos

with sublime passion,
to quiver in the freedom,
a dance of eloquence
for all my wants
and deepest thoughts
these same gifts,
I'd share with you.

Silence Can Heal or Withhold

"What are you thinking?"

She gazed into the iris of his soul and silently queried her understandings.

"Love fades or maybe it never was. Truth stings when lies evolve. Silence can heal or withhold. Words ache when unheard. Passion is voided unless it is real. Trust is delicately earned."

She blinked, blaming the sun's light for her misty eyes and replied,

"Not much."

And swallowed the key to her heart.

Remember

Maybe there's battles we fight and there's ghosts and villains of memories present and past. Maybe it's a cross-section, a generational nightmare and our soul and bones ache with the cadence of voices.

Remember, I believe you.

Maybe there's a twist down a lonely dark path or a spiral into a waterspout above a tangerine sea. Where we sink and fall and soar with feathers and not and pillows protect and hands hold the center of gravity.

Remember, you are not alone.

Maybe the apparitions are not real, but they are to you—a paradox of distinct and faded shadows. It's the mirroring of blue and ash of rising sun star in the riverbanks and channels of the mind's creative eye.

Remember, I see you.

Maybe we have days when up seems down and sideways is but a chance to fly. We wear a cape and a pirate's hat and wield swords of tinfoil and walk with swagger.

Remember, I'll go with you.

Maybe today feels endless but yesterday was joyful and tomorrow we won't know until we step into the sun's rise.

Remember, I am there for you.

Let's find the path of up and down and sideways. Let's hold an hourglass and pour the sand between the souls of warm and sip the sea and swim. Let's love who we are and honor the quirks, next to the logic and saddle up with the fears and self-doubts.

Let's run with our worries and joys and parachute with the colors of our incredible multiplicity of being our self. The magic of our inner childlike is in the awe of pretend. It's in the gift of dreams we have to translate the storms of real. There we see the imagination of answers to the quests we have within.

Remember, I will always believe in you.

"Every secret of a writer's soul, every experience of [her] life, every quality of [her] mind, is written large in [her] words."

—Virginia Woolf

CHAPTER 5

Shadows and Light Are Her Whole

"On the day when it will be possible for woman to love not in her weakness but in strength, not to escape herself but to find herself, not to abase herself but to assert herself—on that day love will become for her, as for [humankind], a source of life..."
—Simone de Beauvoir

She is a Woman

At first, I heard her speak softly in the corner of the room. Her hair was the color of wind and rain. Robin's egg of blue, touched flecks of gray, and streams ran wild under transparent skin. Mountains appeared in her eyes an inner terrain of life lived. The past chapters had laid a foundation—stronger than 10,000 men.

She crept to the center of new and spun a circle of endless. In her heart she just knew; it was time to once again stretch her soul's wings. Each symbolic feather reverberating the sun and the moon. The sea sprung from her heart and her mind touched a shore of stars.

Celestial channels opened to a spiral of seeing beyond the edges of said ordinary; an infinite exchange of awareness and creativity. The crux of the message reverberated her soul's voices of ancient and each was heard to abide by a loving inner revolution. She realized her capacity to make a difference wasn't and isn't a fallacy.

She is integral to the links of humanity and her distinct gifts are as necessary as the sun which rises and the moon that holds light in the night's sky. She bridges the dark of our depths to release the untold; the mystery of our dreams and the ability to see we are all needed.

For she is a woman. Steadfast in her own birthright to receive respect and promulgate justice.

Hot Silence

Walk with me
through my hot silence
as leaves cry
and acid rain burns.

I'll pray waves
to coiled ferns
and reach for bleeding hearts;
moss, is the footstep of
said sounds of needed solace

Hear me,
while I breathe
through punctured hell's thoughts
liken to deaden vines;
I'm seeking kept promises
of more than clematis' new growth.

See me,
become safer
in the quotations of
a breeze
only then
can you understand
why.

I Carry All the Colors

I share all the colors I carry. Sometimes,
melancholy stumbles over an edge
anxiety rises, a sharp gut punch
the randomness, all but blinds
fear spikes a delicate heart
air, sucked from the light
an emotional headlock
chains scream of tears
but no one can hear
an hourglass, lays
on its side, afraid
of where to go
when terror
is dark and
she is all
alone.

Things I love...

I love the way sunlight escapes and rain permeates and puddles create an imaginary space. How closed eyes see and can smell miles of sea— *That half-gaze of sweetness in a starry daydream.*

I love quiet mornings before I am fully awake. How dreams still linger on wrinkled sheets—I think they are folded thoughts delayed in time.

I love walking with stories carried beneath ageless cobblestones —café tables and hearing and being the mélange of languages passing by. For some reason I'm pulled towards conflicts of real and the unfolding of all our feels.

I love the gift of mistakes to understand the why and who of *I-and-you-and-we.* The comfort of tiny naps sandwiched in sunspots of rinsing evergreens. I love how there's often more in less and somehow, someway, kindness, always, always makes a difference—*however small.*

I love subtle nuances and eye-smiles and *soft-sad-real-joy-tears* sharing the hidden of heart.

I need to hear and listen and question just about everything. I don't want to ever stop learning and caring and feeling.

These are some of the things I love.

Our Soul's Innate Brilliance

It's not always the amount of words
but the depth they carry;
the sobs of silence
are weighted
in a chemistry of layered leaves
placed on the stab wounds
of deaf centuries.

I believe,
we are birthed from a golden ratio
of timeless truth;
it is our sacred pureness.

Our fears,
such menacing shadows
are the alloy of a
teacher and friend.
We can relearn.

I'd cross more than rivers
to be by your side
to listen and exchange
what is;
be it sadness or joy
anger or pain
we are the remains
and a reflection
of our truest nature.

"The strength of a woman is not measured by the impact that all her hardships in life have had on her; but the strength of a woman is measured by the extent of her refusal to allow those hardships to dictate her and who she becomes."

—C. JoyBell C.

An Artist's Eye

I want to touch each pixel and feel the colors of holy. Where gray is filtered and drenched in ocean sprays, while wafted clouds are dipped in soul.

I comb through brownish beaches to see the depth of our earth's pained core. It morphs into bizarre and I can barely breathe anymore.

I hold my silent mug of sacredness. It's a touchstone of something real and watch as shocking ruby roses skirt the voice of ancient amethyst sages. My thoughts are a trilogy of blues, until I hear an epiphany from emerald pine trees.

I taste the crunch of air while acknowledging light has turned to ash. It is the salt and rind of our ancestor's bones painted humbly, each night, as weathered weary stars in a vast skyward sea.

I walk through an archive of an artist's naked eye where hues quiver of a hummer's wings and time converts to a sloth's breath.

Here I express my fears, "What the hell is wrong with me to think these things before the sun has shared its warmth with a splash of watered sky?"

I push aside those condemning worries and close, close, close my eyes. There I hold onto each pixel and feel the full curve of space. I've entered into the circles of my deeper soul's embrace.

Watch With Me

Let's watch
as twilight
fades
and stars
become
silent wings
of night and
peace.

Uneasy

It might lift,
the heaviness
the breath of cement
shadows disintegrate
into eerie and endless.

It will ease,
where creases only deepen
rest discovered in tiny branches
on mossy bough to avoid
voices of interrogation.

It's truly fickle,
these variations of shadow
crossing bridges of empty
an unknown destination
of trusting hellish.

Betrayal still lashes
a fierce wound
of grieving stories
burnt pages
memories are awakened;
it's tragic rewriting a worn pattern
and terrifying to see expansion anew

And still,
the fickle unease
will settle
into a looking glass
outward because
inward and surreal will taste real.

Healing is subtle
sometimes jolting
as the walk with soul's water
seeks and discovers new

"I want to get more comfortable being uncomfortable. I want to get more confident being uncertain. I don't want to shrink back just because something isn't easy. I want to push back, and make more room in the area between I can't and I can. Maybe that spot is called I will."

—Kristin Armstrong

My Camera's Focus

I gathered under
a wisp
of crisp moon
my mug,
quickly cold
I forgot time
my feet wet
I forgot shoes

Click
Adjust
Click
Walk
Focus

Camera held to breast.

Stay clear of mind,
in the bluish first light
the rustle of critters
the joy-call of squirrels.

She's here!

The hoot of an owl
I bowed
with the blink
of my eyes
and worshiped the moss,
prayed to the moon
and listened
to the soft crescendo
brush against mine.

Genuine

Genuine, much like compassion, is a quality that radiates from the soul. Its consistency is fluid. There's a current and heart is the epicenter. There's a softness and yet it is powerful and kind.

Realness is at the core. Respect for others is pure.

Even at the pinnacle of silence, genuineness has an expansive quality; a knowing space of vulnerability and courage. It sees. It is deeply felt in the exchange of eye thoughts. The nod of understanding. The sigh of body.

Genuineness is a reflection of walking inside-out.

To meet genuineness is an incredible release and freedom to be at ease. It's rather magical when conversations can ride on waves of profundity as well as silly.

Genuineness is schooled not in degrees or knowledge or material wealth. It is not about achievements. It is an ethereal intelligence; genuineness emanates from soul to soul and sees all beings for the magnificent gifts of our true self.

Just for This Moment

Maybe,
just for this moment,
I'll stay with joyful
and feel her splendor;
the colors awash
in golds and scarlets
of fallen leaves.

I'll open the mist
of morning fog
and hold the rapture
of self-forgiving.
I'll push aside the mountains
calling me down
the well-worn trail of always.

For in this moment,
I'll breathe gratitude.
The scent of gray mixes
with the soft of hush.
The light lingers
on the fringe of dark.

In this moment,
I will honor what is
and what is not.
I'll walk along
the fence of past
and glide to nature's
cathedral of stained glass.

In this moment of repose,
I'll hear the angels of birds

and squirrel chatter sing.
It is like no other.

For in this moment,
I will feel the spaciousness
of joyful and just be.

Tiny Moments of Real

Some things can't be taught. They have to be felt so we can really see. Sometimes in the quietest spaces we hear and know more truth than a lot of talk. Respect is built on consistency. Inner wisdom is the kiln of some of the finer shades of insight. Sometimes trusting isn't easy but with practice it gets easier.

No, means exactly that.

Stop, does too.

Intelligence without empathy misses the point.

It is in these tiny moments, when I get a glimpse and know I'm touching another segment of my soul.

I write because sentences have structure and paragraphs hold an ethereal realm between the letters and words. Writing has fluidity, logic, clarity, a visual sketch of mind and a place to release so much. It often baffles and also comforts me.

Heart-Stretching

The process of a heart-stretch is an emotional and spiritual profundity. With each soulful expansion there are subtle shifts of shedding and unraveling.

It's a profound process between exhaustion and quiet respect.

When we devote the time and waves of energy to the process of self-exploration, we are not only enhancing our inner growth but we contribute to a generational healing.

Heart-stretching touches a common ground of oneness. Its rippled influences are felt at a cellular level. Listening and nonjudgmental acknowledgment are acquired.

With the delicate stitches of empathy, coupled with a blend of harmonizing trust, we can fill the once silenced chapters with necessary kindness, wisdom and unpretentious love.

It is my vision to continue the path of personal heart-stretching and to equally absorb the flexible sequences to provide a healing space for the heart-stretch of others.

Silence

Sounds are muffled
in the stillness
of a feverishly
cold morn
and my thoughts
get less tangled
in the tide pools
of acquitted
self-reflection.

Love, Grief and Cobblestones

I spent years walking the cobblestones of faraway lands. Lyrical lush languages were spoken on the tongues of heart. We had young memories and laughs, promises and hopes; but compassion was a dream for reality spoke.

Truth isn't always lovely. And lies will corrode; it rips at the seams of confidence.

At night—to breathe—I wore the weave of owl's feathers and soared against a blackened sky. I danced with spirits for I didn't realize love was amiss. I felt dead and didn't know why.

It wasn't until my feet reached the shores and I walked for days with the wind and wonder of waves. The sea befriended me. Only then could I understand the well of my cobblestoned grief.

The sea spray and I wept, I heard my soul whisper,

"You are enough. Just as you are. It's time to follow your heart."

Love isn't when we become more or different or prettier or change into someone else. Love bends and gives and recognizes the faults as well as the wrinkles of wisdom. Love wraps the comfort of unwinding the mysteries and crosses with the bridges of dawn and night.

I see now, it's better to be alone than to pretend.

An Artist's Mosaic

Maybe,
when an artist creates a mosaic
they are taking shattered pieces of self
and rearranging the pain into art.

Maybe,
the kiln of despair
cures the brokenness
and burns off
another layer so we can see clearer.

Let's hold the tenderness
of shadow's truths
because there's wisdom
deep in our scars.

Let's wrap a blanket
around the spirits
haunting the crevices
of our unknown.

Let's rest in the knowing
this is the unveiling
and trajectory of being;
a healing and seeing
the path of our heart.

Compassion

Compassion spoke
with subtle notes of pure,
so soft,
I almost missed it.

I closed my eyes
to witness
the interconnectedness of life.

Wind spoke.
Trees bowed.
Morning filled branches with song.
Sunlight crested each blade of grass;
a harp of lyrical delicateness.

The dawn of day.
The prayer shawl of night.
The dance of magic—an elliptical sequence.

I began to tremble in the flow.
I became a mountain.
My soul planted in moss and streams.
Deer rested.
Birds chortled seamlessly.
Whales breached through the saline.

I connected with the compassion of Mother Earth
and she willingly received me.
We flew together
in endless space
to touch the tips of stars.
We navigated riptides
and rested in warm tidal pools.

No words were spoken
but profoundly sensed.
Compassion touched me
in my frail tenderness.

Remind Me

Remind me when the sun rests it will still rise
and the moon sometimes needs to hide
and *it's okay—not to be okay*
I'll dwell in the arms of a tree.

Remind me when lavender gets wild with age
it's fine to let her flow freely
much like rose petals fall
to adorn the thorny ankles of her cane.

Remind me when sadness thwarts my perception
a clearing will follow the tempest
and imagination will once again spin
from fibers delicate as the bud of dancing lupine.

Remind me how sipping warmth is a liquid embrace
and daydreaming is not a useless affair
it is the wings of a butterfly as it caresses flora
and graces life and honors the death of despair.

Remind me to be still in the sound of silence
and to unfold inside a spiraled shell of respite
where the sound of love extends
and softens the core of my rocky shore.

Remind me I am loved especially when I feel not so;
to cherish the strong silvery locks of wisdom
and to favor my extra creases of said certainty,
learning how age releases and I befriend my inner foes.

Remind me I need to wander freely
on grassy knolls and drift like an untamed river
especially when my spirit hurts;
encourage me to walk until the path of my creativity returns.

Remind me how slumber sounds like waves
and tears are the eyelashes of the sea and
how love reaches beyond the shores and
how the deepest beauty is felt and not
always what it seems.

Sea Sick

It isn't necessarily a bad thing to feel all the time; she brushed with emotions as if they were air. Sometimes though, it was difficult to navigate when a clash of fears erupted beneath her eyes.

Sea sick from a riptide, she navigated blindly into depths still married to shame and imprinted on the skin of her antiquity.

Noting the severity of the deep dive, she deliberately pulled herself over rocks and sought a channel of gentle. And there it was—tucked in sun-warmed, and teeming with tender—she found silence and birthed a reflection of naked self-love and worth.

Depth of Our Tide's Knowing

The veil,
is joy of light and
wings of solemn sanctuary
its flight
a wisp of soundless threads
and voice of dancing spirits
a sojourn
of ethereal and earth
hearts parched to understand
slate upon sand
sea upon edges
and a depth of tide's knowing
a walk
between sheer and listen
the message is,
to love.

She Was More Than Blue

She wasn't just blue. She sang the blues and felt every shade of blue—indigo and sometimes cerulean or azure. The depth of her blueness was adaptable and constantly shifting.

Skimming the surface—impossible.

Her perspective could be a stormy sea, with bluish skin but the ability to breathe fire.

She redefined obstacles. Her smoldering rage towards injustices leaked through with precision. She recreated blue and became a fire. She hotwired her fuses and tripped the circuit breakers. She had to. The skeleton of empty lies, brokenness and deceit were a vacant graveyard.

With growing awareness, she used each as a stepping stone to rebuild. Failure became synonymous with strength. Betrayal's swelling of disenchantment was unplugged and replaced with self-trust.

Deliberately, she turned negativity inside-out and shined light on the blues and reconnected to her soul-speak. Respecting her inner quest of much needed solitude; and still, speaking her truth.

Dear Tender Self,

You are an unsent letter wrapped in an ancient envelope. A tea-stained seal never fully closed. Calligraphy etches on the onionskin of your sensitivities. Each layer of you is unraveling swiftly. It is necessary to find the crease of rest in the trifold of expansion.

You are not lost.
Healing is a passage of timelessness.
Rest in a sampling of moss; it is always dear and true.

Let yourself soar through fields of dreams and see symbols rise in the wake of storms. See the now, held tenderly onto the stream of precious processing. An abundant wealth of wisdom resides in the textured layers of your story. Let your mind braid lavender wands and rest in the nook of an evergreen. Lean into the wind and anchor into the crevices of a rock. Become flora and bend to the universe. Let the inner you be gently swayed. Resting is more than okay. It is necessary.

The rings of your story connect with wisdom's growth and forever speak to the pillars of the earth. Melt into the colors of driftwood washed upon the shores of your daydreams. Find rhythm of your voice. Let the sandy grains of yesterday fade and teach well. See the shadows as teachers and let the star of inner light guide; for all of this is your voice.

She Knew

With every breath
she went
a little deeper
by letting her light
into the spaces
shutdown
like a seed germinating
in the pocket of her heart
she was ready to grow
even more.

A Stained Glass Heart

The images fell
like slivers of stained glass

She gathered each colorful slice
and laid out an abstract configuration

Forgoing the obvious
and letting the rules slip away

She gathered strength from knowing
and ignored the critics

She snipped the tattered stitches from brokenness
and let fresh chords play harmony into the spaces

She stood in the thickest part of her
heart and rearranged her perspective

Closing her eyes,
she let nature speak,

"What you are is beautiful
your wings are boundless,
a semi-circle of luminescence,
let your voice be heard."

Her vision expanded
into an arching aura
she closed her eyes
to see a stained glass window
etched with the words:

It takes time to create a masterpiece.

Moods and Restless Nights

I write on a similar path as the moon caresses the sky. She shows herself to me.

My emotions and thoughts tempered as much by her shadows as her light. I hold with deep respect the changes of my femininity.

Age is also playing a role as I see myself step into her truth and find her voice. It is through these temperate transitions of tenacious insights, I write.

The moon is at half and I feel her growing energies within.

I learn from the split of dark and light. Peace comes from facing and untangling our shadows.

I watch the moon as nature's candle light; it glows an inordinate amount of wisdom.

I listen and feel and learn to follow her guidance. She has mastered the tides of the sea and has much to teach me. There's always something magical when I look to the sky and know, we all share a stellar cloak of the heavens. This comforts me.

We Are All Sides of Our Story

The courage it takes to fully embrace all of our story, brings me to my vulnerable knees. To bear witness of others doing the same, I bow at their sanctity. And once we start this epic journey, I realize there is no turning back.

The layers keep revealing an endless depth of visceral healing. My story overlaps into yours and creates an embroidered fabric. All stitches are necessary.

As we surround our self, with the insightful intuitiveness of learning how to love and to be loved, we gain the trust to hold and can mix our teachings into new. The spectrum is infinite.

We inevitably create support by bearing witness to it all. It is no longer a monopoly of who is right or wrong. In this process, when we have been seen for who we are and the gifts we each carry—we grow, share and change. Our shadows of shame, abuse, anxieties, violence, fears and worries join in with a reciprocity of joy, healing, love, peace and acceptance.

There's an immense relief when our intellect can create a union with soul. It is in this precious space, all pretense fades and we finally see and believe who we truly are.

ABOUT THE AUTHOR

Carolyn (Riker) Avalani, MA, LMHC, is a teacher, counselor, writer and poet. In 1992, Carolyn completed her graduate studies in Psychological Services & Counseling, from Marymount University, Arlington VA. She pursued post-graduate studies at Johns Hopkins, Baltimore, MD and became a Licensed Professional Counselor in 1994. After moving to Seattle, WA in 1996, she became a Licensed Mental Health Counselor. Her poetry and essays have appeared namely in *Women's Spiritual Poetry* Blog, *Rebelle Society*, *elephant journal*, and four anthologies.

Carolyn worked for several years as a Psychiatric Counselor with a local hospital in Virginia. Additionally, she volunteered as an advocate for women and children of domestic violence, and provided crisis intervention, education and support. Later she became a Domestic Relations Counselor for the 18th District Court in Alexandria, VA. For the next three years she provided her expertise on court ordered counseling and mediation for families of domestic violence.

Leaving the east coast, in 1996 and moving to the Seattle area, Carolyn became a therapist for a nonprofit counseling organization as well as a private school counselor. In addition to individual and couples counseling, she facilitated creative writing workshops.

Carolyn is currently in private practice offering counseling, journal writing workshops and creative writing services via phone, Skype or Zoom.

More information is available at www.carolynriker.com.

ADDENDUM

The following poems have been previously published in these publications:

Message of the Birds, published in *Journey of the Heart: An Anthology of Spiritual Poetry by Women*.

Feathers of Morning (originally *Be Still*), published in *Poetry as a Spiritual Practice: Illuminating the Awakened Woman*.

Winter is My Companion, published with *Women's Spiritual Poetry*.

Moon Nectar, published in *Poetry as a Spiritual Practice: Illuminating the Awakened Woman*.

We Are Love, published in *Where Journeys Meet: The Voice of Women's Poetry*.

Inner Voice, published in *Where Journeys Meet: The Voice of Women's Poetry*.

A Love Story in 108 Words, published with *elephant journal*.

Read Me Like Braille, published with *Women's Spiritual Poetry*.

Remind Me, published with *Women's Spiritual Poetry*.

Dear Tender Self, published with *Women for One*.

A Stained Glass Heart, published in *Where Journeys Meet: The Voice of Women's Poetry*.